$\mathcal{T}$able of Contents

$\mathcal{I}$ntroduction

INTRODUCTION

Good communication skills are fundamental to all relationships and your key to business success. How you communicate your thoughts and feelings to others and how you manage your differences are predictors of the quality of your relationships at home or at the office. When individuals don't speak clearly, listen accurately, or assert themselves effectively, the result is reduced profit, diminished self-esteem and lowered company morale. The purpose of this book is to provide you with ways to enhance your communication skills and increase your effectiveness.

People need to be able to call upon a sophisticated set of interpersonal skills to reach their communication goals and to help others reach theirs. This book is designed to facilitate practical communication skills that complement teamwork, interdependence and shared responsibility, which are the benchmarks of successful businesses and corporations today.

Chapter 1 defines communication and addresses poor communication skills. It discusses the differences and interconnections of reading, listening, speaking and writing.

The purpose of communication is to share information. What you say is only as effective and informative as how it's heard. Recent studies show that men and women hear and communicate differently. Chapter 2 addresses the problems in gender communication and shows how men and women speak and hear differently. It offers you techniques to improve understanding between men and women.

Listening ranks as the most valuable communication skill. Whether it's between men and women or it takes the form of reading, writing and speaking, listening is at the very heart of good communication. We assume listening comes naturally when, in fact, it is a learned activity. Chapter 3 offers techniques for *reflective listening* to improve your listening skills. Reflective listening helps you focus on the central points of the speaker's message and helps the speaker stay on the topic. It also allows him to vent his emotions so he can move toward a solution. This chapter includes both *psychological listening* and *physical listening* and offers advice on drawing the speaker out and inviting him to vent his feelings on safe ground.

Listening is an art that involves your whole body. The section dealing with *physical listening* shows how to assume a posture and attitude of silent responsiveness. A lifetime of poor communication habits, while difficult to undo, can be improved with work and practice. The goal is to be on good terms with all people, and, at the same time, maintain your own dignity and self-worth. How you and your employees present yourselves to others gives them an image of your company. What image are you trying to portray?

Chapter 4 deals with assertiveness and offers techniques to achieve this valuable communication skill. It offers the four-part assertiveness communication formula and describes effective assertion messages.

You don't need a college education or a big vocabulary to communicate assertively. Often, it's not what you say, but how you say it. Chapter 5 examines non-verbal communication and considers such key components as eye contact, body posture, facial expression, gestures, vocal tone, inflection and volume as well as fluency, timing and clothing. All make positive or negative statements about you and affect the way you are perceived by others.

Chapter 6 discusses public speaking and shows how to organize and arrange your speech into three main parts. Time is the underlying consideration of giving a speech. This chapter discusses timing and offers tips on writing, arranging and rehearsing your speech to obtain maximum effectiveness.

Writing is another form of communication. Good writing grabs the reader's attention and persuades, influences and sells the ideas of your company. Chapter 7 offers advice and asks questions to help you get the most from the least number of words. It gives advice for all your writing needs and provides thought patterns for good writing.

Because many of us are uncomfortable with compliments, Chapter 8 offers practical advice on how to accept them. More of us have trouble accepting criticism, and most view it as a personal rejection. Chapter 8 deals with compliments and criticism and puts them in their proper perspectives. It offers techniques to help you accept compliments and criticism gracefully and, at the same time, leave your self-esteem intact.

We have all been in work situations where feelings and emotions escalate. Chapter 9 focuses on *problem-solving* and *conflict resolution*. It describes Bolton's six-step Collaborative Problem-Solving Method and makes us aware of stumbling blocks to avoid while pointing out the benefits of this technique.

Chapter 10 continues the theme by addressing the problem of anger in the workplace and offers ways of dealing with it. It tells when the best strategy is to avoid, accommodate, compromise, compete or negotiate. You will learn which strategies to use when. This chapter teaches you how to evaluate conflict. It shows how to handle problems and resolve conflict to enrich relationships.

What differentiates the effective person from the ineffective person? What makes us like some persons and not others? Chapter 11 discusses charisma and teaches you how to match sensory modes and use parallelism to increase your *charisma quotient*. It shows you how to make others feel they are in sync with you and speaking on the same wavelength.

As we conclude this century, no communication skills handbook is complete without a chapter on the Internet. Chapter 12 brings you to the cutting edge of high tech's electronic medium. It introduces you to the Information Superhighway and to the living concept of the virtual office. It explains how to use e-mail, faxing and voice mail to cut time and costs. It discusses new ways of conducting business, interviewing potential employees, even conferencing with other branches of your company in other parts of the world via Internet Relay Chat.

You can learn new and effective communication skills. At no other time in the history of big business and giant corporations, with its emphasis on leadership and team responsibility, has good communication been more stressed. This book offers you the means to attain these skills and put them into practice in your own company. Each chapter links to the next, allowing ease of movement from one interconnecting communication skill to the other. Now is the time for you and your company to incorporate the skills of successful companies all over the world.

WHAT IS COMMUNICATION

"For it is not upon the physical sciences that the future will depend. It is upon us who are trying to understand and deal with the interactions between human beings."

—Carl Rogers

When Clement Haynesworth was nominated to fill a vacancy on the Supreme Court, most people agreed he was a mediocre candidate. In their opinion, he had been a mediocre lawyer and a mediocre judge. Roman Hruska, in arguing for Haynesworth's appointment, remarked in complete seriousness that since there were so many mediocre people in America, they were entitled to be represented by a mediocre Supreme Court Justice.

Referring to a recent vote in Canada for Quebec's separation, Quebec Prime Minister Jacques Parizeau attributed the loss of the vote to "money and the ethnic vote". One wonders whose money, and which Canadians were the "ethnic" voters?

These are examples of "stupid talk" in the political arena. Professor Neil Postman defines "stupid talk" as talk that has a confused direction, an inappropriate tone or a vocabulary not well suited to its context. Such talk does not and cannot achieve its purposes.

We find "stupid talk" in our own lives as well. Susan once remarked to her co-worker, Hank, that he would have to be "blind, deaf and dumb" not to understand Susan's comments during a recent business meeting. To her dismay, Susan learned that Hank's wife was blind and he was very offended by the comment.

Fred often berates his employee, Stephanie, because she is "always" late and "never" on time, rather than constructively dealing with the conflict her frequent tardiness is causing. His "stupid talk" is an avoidance technique, enabling him to delay an inevitable confrontation.

Messages bounce off the moon, and space probes land on Mars. Yet, speaking is still troublesome for most of us. Words reflect what fills the heart. What do your words tell others about you? Imagine you are being introduced for the first time to a large group of people from a competitor's company. Perhaps rumor, gossip and misrepresentation preceded you. When communication is blocked or muddled, relationships wither and eventually die. However, conflict, cruelty and misunderstanding can be conquered through effective communication. When open, clear communication takes place, relationships and cooperation flourish. Once you develop good communication skills, you can choose the way you communicate with, and influence, others. It will be up to you to change the mind of individuals, as well as the crowd. During a debate over the national budget, Senator Hollings of South Carolina commented, "A million here ... a million there ... and pretty soon it adds up to REAL money." To hardworking Americans, a million dollars *is* "real" money.

The success of an organization depends on the communication skills of its employees. When 170 organizations were asked their primary reason for rejecting an applicant, inability to communicate and poor communication skills were mentioned most frequently. People who polished oral and written communication skills advance more rapidly and contribute more fully to their organizations. No matter how much expertise you have in your chosen profession, your communication skills can make the difference between great success and simply "getting by." Most work problems can be traced back to a failure in communication.

Sarah, a civil engineer laments, "I thought my engineering training was all I would need, but I spend most of my time on people problems." Norman, a beautician, also observes, "I was trained to do hair. Since I've been on the job, I not only fix hair, I have to fix people." Your communication style is a learned response. Unfortunately, most of us learned poor communication skills from well-intentioned people.

This book offers skills to develop and support business communication. Three principles underlie these chapters:

> 1. Communication is a learned behavior.
>
> 2. You can make a significant difference in the quality of your interpersonal relationships through improved communication.
>
> 3. When you practice, you perfect new skills.

To improve communication, we must understand exactly what it is. The Latin root of the word *communicate* is *communicare* which means to make common or to share.

The purpose of communication, therefore, is to express thoughts, ideas and feelings with others in a way they will understand. Good communication has little to do with a large vocabulary. It has everything to do with making yourself understood.

How do you make contact with other people? How do they respond to you? Sometimes they respond through facial expressions, gestures or other body signals, but mostly it is through the use of language — writing and speaking on the one hand; reading and listening on the other.

Writing and reading go together, as do speaking and listening. Writing is meaningless until it is read. You might as well shout into the wind if what you say is unheard. Instruction in writing and reading starts in elementary school and continues through college. Except for special courses in public speaking and help for those with speech defects, formal education provides no instruction for speaking and listening. We assume that communication skills come naturally and no training is required.

Poor reading and writing skills are common targets of criticism. Yet, training a person in reading and writing does not teach him how to speak and listen. Speaking and listening differ vastly from reading and writing.

The reason for this is the fluidity of oral communication. When you read, you have the option of rereading for clarity. When you write, you can rewrite. Speaking and listening are transient. They are as fleeting as the performance of a creative artist.

A writer hopes that readers will take the time to understand the written message, but the speaker cannot have such hope. He must present the message in a clear, understandable way. Effective written and verbal communication are learned skills. Many of us inherited ineffective, self-defeating communication skills. All of us are guilty of "stupid talk" at various times in our lives. By learning to recognize and correct the weak spots in our personal communication styles, we take an important step toward increased effectiveness. We take a large step toward making ourselves understood.

Key Concepts in Chapter 1

- "Stupid talk" is talk with a confused direction, an inappropriate tone or a vocabulary that is not well-suited to its content. It is talk that does not and cannot achieve its purposes.

- Communication is a learned behavior.

- You can significantly improve the quality of your interpersonal communication.

- With practice, you can give your communication an appropriate direction and tone.

1. Think about the Latin word, *communicare*, which means to make common or to share. Think of communication as a sharing. Then it becomes important to be aware of how you communicate. To begin building your communication skills, notice how people receive your words.

2. Listen for evidence of "stupid talk." If you hear yourself using stupid talk, replay the conversation and determine what you could have said instead.

3. Identify the weak spots in your communication. What would you like to improve?

4. Make a tape recording of your voice and listen to yourself. Do you use language effectively? What do you like about the way you speak? What do you dislike?

Reflections

WHAT DID YOU SAY? GENDER SPEAK IN THE WORKPLACE

"What is the solution, then, if men and women are talking at cross purposes ...? How are we to open lines of communication? The answer is for both men and women to try to take each other on their own terms rather than applying the standards of one group over another."

—Deborah Tannen

Even with the success of the women's liberation movement and the increase in the number of women in the work force, girls and boys are still educated by society to speak and act differently. When young boys swear and use tough language, their behavior is tolerated as normal for their age. We assume they are trying to act big. Grown men pepper their vocabulary with occasional profanity and it is acceptable. No corresponding freedom exists for women and little girls. Verbally and physically, female actions are expected to be more restrained than their male counterparts. This directly affects the communication skills of both females and males. At work, we often find ourselves at cross purposes.

But, whether male/female differences stem from genetic makeup, parental influence or cultural conditioning by society, the fact is we are different. We act differently. We speak differently. Men often assume a direct, forceful manner of communicating, while women typically acquire a quieter, more tentative, questioning approach. The result of these differing uses of language often leads to misunderstandings. John Gray,

7

whom has contributed much to our understanding of the communication styles of men and women, says that by accepting and validating these male and female differences, we can begin to close the communication gap.

The first step is to accept our differences. Different doesn't mean wrong. Men tend to define themselves through their achievements. They like to handle things on their own. So at work, if a woman suggests to a man that he ask for help, he may think she believes he is inept or, worse, incompetent.

Women define who they are through the connectedness of their relationships and through feelings. Reverse the above situation, and the woman would not as likely take offense at the suggestion. Much of our business communication is based upon the interpretation of the male and female listener. Words are only as useful as the way they are heard.

The second step is to learn the rules of communication. We have rules for just about everything we do. When we engage in sports, we play by the rules; when we drive, we follow the rules of safe driving, when we play games, we play according to the rules. We even have the Golden Rule. Learn the rules that men follow when they communicate. Seek to understand the rules women also unconsciously follow for successful communication.

For communication between men and women to be effective, we must recognize the differences between male and female communication styles. Men and women, at home or in the workplace, whether speaking or listening, use communication methods designed to meet their primary communication needs.

Men's Needs	Women's Needs
1. to feel accepted	1. to feel validated
2. to feel admired	2. to feel respected
3. to feel appreciated	3. to feel understood
4. to feel approved of	4. to feel reassured
5. to feel trusted	5. to feel cared about

For Men

Kathy needs time off one afternoon this week for a doctor appointment. A lump was found that is concerning her. However, her fear of asking Tom for the time off is greater than her fear of what the doctor may discover. In the past Tom has pushed her aside whenever requests for personal time have been made, discrediting her needs as mere excuses to play hooky. She would like to think, as her employer, that Tom would be concerned about her health, but wonders just how much of her own anxiety she is free to share.

The No. 1 way a man can improve his communication skills with a women is by listening to her feelings. This may not be easy since he is coming from a different perspective.

The first thing a man should do is to keep in mind how quickly unpleasant feelings can arise in a conversation he feels is going well. These feelings come from not listening with an understanding of the woman's point of view. For good gender communication to take place, a man must start taking the responsibility for understanding the way women talk.

Don't blame her for upsetting you. Her feelings are valid even if they don't make sense to you right away. Before coming to conclusions, try to see the situation through her eyes. Keep in mind a woman's primary communication needs and use your conversation to make her feel validated, respected and understood. Take the time to reassure her and let her know you care about what she is saying. Make her feel that you are listening to her and your communication will improve.

Sometimes males experience uncomfortable emotions because they do not know what to do to solve things. To improve business communications, men must learn to resist the urge to take the problem completely off a female counterpart's shoulders. Don't offer more solutions. Because women talk about problems does not mean they don't know the solutions. Women want men to listen to them.

To have good communication with women, you don't have to always agree with them. If you disagree, however, you'll be better able to get your point across if you wait until they are finished talking. Men often try to talk over each other when they disagree. They raise their voices and interrupt each other. Women interpret these actions as power plays, and communication suffers.

Also, don't pretend to understand when you don't, and don't automatically start defending yourself. You communicate better with women if you admit when you don't understand. If you disagree and feel strongly about the issue, let women know that what they said is important to you. Then gently explain your point of view. If you make a mistake, especially when you have slighted her feelings, apologize. If you listen and acknowledge her feelings, you'll close the gender gap and open the door to effective business communications.

For Women

David enjoys getting feedback from his fellow architect, Sharon. They are working together on designs for a new dental complex. Sharon is a good listener as David goes over the plans, nodding and giving him encouraging comments as he brainstorms ideas with her. Even though she has been with the firm two years longer than David, he never feels she is condescending toward him. Instead, she often tells him he is doing a great job. He notices even when they disagree on a concept, her suggestions for improvements seem to build on his own ideas rather than attack them. As a result, he is very open and eager to include her ideas as well.

Just as men have a problem with listening, women need to empower their male counterparts. Don't ask him too many questions or he may feel you are prying, or trying to change him. He will either become defensive or agree with you for the moment to passify you. When sharing feelings with a man, let him know you are not trying to tell him what to do.

Nowhere is the pause more practically or usefully applied than in gender communication. This gives the listener the opportunity to consider the speaker's primary needs before responding. This is especially useful when a female asks a male for support or a favor. Allow the male to work through his resistance, even if he grumbles. As long as you remain silent you stand a good chance of getting what you asked for. Women have a tendency to break the silence with comments like, "Oh, never mind," or "It's not that important," or "Don't bother."

Women also have a tendency to ask tag questions, with qualifiers. This makes their statements less powerful and believable. Women must learn to avoid saying things like, "That was the most moving speech I ever heard, don't you think?" Adding "don't you think?" makes the statement less powerful and makes you appear unsure of yourself.

Men often talk over women, or speak louder to get their point across. This makes women feel unevenly matched. Worse, it can be interpreted by women as a means of control. The soft spoken, more tentative style common to women, however, can be wrongly interpreted as being uninformed or unsure.

Once you realize that men and women have different conversational styles, you can begin accepting differences without blaming or criticizing. Nothing hurts more than being told you're doing something wrong when you know you are right, or feeling that others think your intentions are bad when you know they're good. Our differences can enrich our lives and show us another dimension to business decisions that we would not know if we were all the same.

Key Concepts in Chapter 2

- Men and women learn to speak differently.

- Men define who they are through their achievements. They believe they are what they do.

- Women define themselves through their connection with others. They believe they are what they feel.

- When speaking with men, remember their need to feel accepted, admired, appreciated, approved and trusted.

- When speaking with women, remember their need to feel validated, respected, understood, reassured and cared about.

- The number one way a man can improve his relationship with a woman is to listen to her feelings.

- The number one way a woman can improve her relationship with a man is to empower him.

1. Take 10 minutes a day and think of the differences in how you speak with members of the opposite sex. If you are a man, do you tend to talk down to a woman? Do you increase your volume to prevent her from entering the conversation? If you are a woman, do you tend to act cute, coy or helpless when you talk to a man?

2. Keep a communication journal. Write down instances of times when you responded to the opposite sex in a way you would not have responded to your own.

3. If you are a man, the next time you are in conversation with women, convey the message that you care about what she is saying. Validate her feelings. Let her know that you respect her. Reassure her if necessary.

   If you a woman, the next time you are in conversation with a man, convey the message that you admire and accept him. Let him know you appreciate him. Make him feel trusted and approved of.

Reflections

3 LISTENING: THE HEART OF COMMUNICATION

> "Real communication occurs when we listen with understanding ... It means to see the expressed idea and attitude from the other person's point of view, to sense how it feels to be him, to achieve his frame of reference in regard to the thing he is talking about."
>
> —*Carl Rogers*

Do you interrupt? How much do you talk? A lot? Not enough? Do you need to have the last word? How well do you listen?

Most of us think we are good listeners. We assume listening comes naturally. However, listening is just as complicated as reading, writing and speaking. Listening requires mental and physical activity. We spend 80 percent of each day listening. Listening is our most frequently used communication skill, yet we often feel that it requires no effort on our part.

Research shows that 40 percent of your professional salary is earned by listening. This percentage increases as you climb the professional ladder. Eighty percent of a CEO's salary is earned listening. Sperry Rand targeted listening as the communication skill it most wants its employees to improve. Sperry spends millions on effective listening training. Management there recognizes that their employees' listening skills are not as effective as they could be, even though listening consumes a major portion of the workday.

Reflective Listening

Skilled listening allows you to step into the other person's shoes and respond appropriately. An appropriate response restates the speaker's feelings and content in a way that demonstrates acceptance and understanding — that reflects what you heard the speaker say. A useful formula for reflecting is this: "You feel (insert the word or feeling) because (insert the event or other content that is associated with the feeling)."

Reflective listening only allows you to focus on the central points of the issue, and keeps the speaker focused.

Reflective listening encourages the other person to disclose his feelings, thereby helping him understand his emotions and move toward a solution to the problem.

As you listen, focus on these areas:

1. Listen for the prevailing emotion. Be aware of the emotional elements that drive the speaker and his perceptions. Pay attention to how feelings are expressed in terms of the actual words used as well as by the speaker's nonverbal communication: his tone, emphasis and body language.

2. Put yourself in the speaker's shoes. See the issue from his standpoint. Take into consideration all you know about this person's business and personal life. Is he confronting several deadlines? Is he experiencing personal stress? This insight will give you a clearer understanding of the speaker's feelings.

Some complain that reflective listening is too structured. When you learn to use it properly, you forget the formula, and reflection becomes natural. Others are skeptical about the feelings that arise when they first begin reflective listening. Awkward and insincere feelings turn into empathy as you practice these skills.

Reflective listening provides a mechanism that draws the other person out. You can do this in several ways:

1. Indicate your interest in the person and what he is saying. This invites him to talk.

2. Don't interrupt, offer an opinion or otherwise prevent the speaker from continuing. Even if the speaker pauses, don't speak. Let him resume the conversation.

3. Involve your whole body. Maintain good eye contact. Nod when the person makes a point.

4. Make listening sounds like, "Hmmm," "Really," "That's interesting," "What do you think about that?" This lets the speaker know you are paying attention.

Physical Listening

Listening involves giving physical attention to the speaker. Listening with your whole body shows your interest in what is being said. Incline your body toward the speaker to communicate more energy and interest. Face the speaker squarely — your right shoulder to his left shoulder — to communicate your involvement in the discussion. When someone says, "He gave me the cold shoulder," they often mean that indifference or rejection was communicated.

To avoid giving someone a cold shoulder, face him squarely at eye level. Your eye contact communicates interest and a desire to listen. Keep your arms and legs uncrossed. Tightly crossed arms or legs communicate defensiveness and closed mindedness. Position yourself at an appropriate distance. If you are too distant or too close, the speaker will feel anxiety. About three feet is a comfortable distance for conversation.

Avoid making distracting motions and gestures, but don't sit too rigidly either. Move your body in response to the speaker. The skilled listener avoids environmental distractions. Turn off the television or stereo. Close the door. In the workplace, have your phone calls held and instruct visitors to wait. Remove the physical barriers. Don't isolate yourself on the opposite side of an executive desk. This only sets up psychological distance and impedes good communication.

Most listeners talk too much. Learn the art of silent responsiveness. A good listener strikes an effective balance of reflective paraphrasing and silent responsiveness. Learning to read body language is an important skill for effective listening because much of interpersonal communication is nonverbal. People sometimes try to conceal their feelings by controlling their nonverbal communication. This usually is not effective. Most often, emotions leak out despite efforts to regulate nonverbal expression. Here are some guidelines to help you read body language.

- Focus attention on: facial expressions, posture, gestures and actions.

- Read nonverbals in context of the conversation.

- Note discrepancies between what people say and how they act. For example, if they say they are happy, do they look and act happy.

- Be aware of your feelings and physical reactions.

Body language sometimes is very clear. Other times, it is difficult to determine. When the listener appropriately reflects his understanding of the other person's body language, communication improves significantly.

Whatever your business or profession, the ability to listen effectively is critical to success. However, improving listening skills is not easy. A lifetime full of poor listening habits is difficult to undo. But with knowledge and practice, you can improve your listening skills. While listening is often a delight, it is also demanding. Listening is primary to all other forms of communication. You must listen in order to learn to speak, read and write. Listening is not a passive activity. Good listening skills are at the heart of effective and meaningful communication.

Key Concepts in Chapter 3

- Listening consumes more of our daily lives than any other communication process.

- Reflective listening restates the feeling and content that the speaker communicated.

- Reflective listening demonstrates that the listener understands and accepts the speaker's message.

- Reflective listening requires observation of nonverbal communication.

- The listener must communicate interest in the speaker through appropriate nonverbal encouragements.

- The effective listener uses only a few well-chosen, open-ended questions to facilitate the speaker's message.

- Responsive silence is a key factor in effective communication.

1. Set aside time to work on your listening skills. Begin by paying attention to how you listen. What does your posture and facial expression say to others? If possible ask a friend to assess your listening habits. In your communication journal, write some goals for how you feel you can improve your listening habits.

2. Practice reflective listening by using the formula, "You feel (insert the feeling) because (insert the event or other content that is associated with the feeling)." Write in your journal how reflective listening makes you feel. Do you feel uncomfortable, insincere, self-conscious? Note changes that occur as you use the formula over time.

3. Make a point to involve your whole body when you listen. Lean toward the speaker. Maintain eye contact.

4. What does the other person's body language say to you? Write your perceptions in your journal.

Reflections

ASSERT YOURSELF

"Our words are often hidden containers of hidden hopes and cloudy expectations. Our silence assumes a power to communicate it does not have. Our timing tires and offends. Whenever we have expectations of others that we do not say directly, we set ourselves up for disappointment."

—*Fran Ferder*

Are you comfortable talking with people you don't know? Do you dread saying no? Do you allow strangers to cut you off in the cafeteria line? Do you regret stepping on others to achieve your goals? Do you feel you get your needs across to others?

Your words and behavior tell people who you are. Human communication and behavior fall into three basic categories:

- Passiveness
- Aggressiveness
- Assertiveness

Passiveness is a reluctance or inability to confidently express what you think and feel. In the past, our society rewarded women for being passive and men for being aggressive. Fortunately, as more and more women voice their concerns in the workplace, this is changing.

Aggressive communication and behavior, whether direct or indirect, results in a put-down of the other person, making her feel hurt, defensive and humiliated. Aggressive behavior does not take the other person's goals or feelings into account. Only the aggressor's goals are met. This often generates bitterness and frustration that later returns as resistance and dissension. Think of a time when someone used aggressive communication at the expense of another person. How would you feel about approaching such a person? Aggression intimidates, demeans and degrades another person. It also degrades the aggressor.

Assertiveness is an alternative to the extremes of passiveness and aggressiveness. Norma Carr-Ruffino defines assertion as "confidently expressing what you think, feel and believe — standing up for your rights while respecting the rights of others."

Assertion is rooted in respect: respect for yourself and for the other person. People tend to cooperate when they are approached or advised in a way that respects the needs of both parties. Assertive communication frequently allows both persons to get what they want.

Assertive behavior is self-enhancing. When you express your feelings honestly, you usually achieve your goal. When you choose to behave in an assertive manner, even if your goals are not achieved, you generally feel good about yourself.

It's true that you must tailor your communication to circumstances of each new situation. Behavior that applies to some persons and circumstances does not apply to all persons or situations. Each situation is different. Sometimes a passive response is most appropriate. Sometimes, an aggressive response is needed. Most of the time, assertiveness is the key.

The ultimate goal is to be on good terms with people. Be true to your own thoughts, feelings and beliefs. Avoid direct or implied criticism of the other person's thoughts, feelings or beliefs, and you are likely to retain the goodwill of those around you. Think in terms of I-messages. An I-message expresses your feelings and experiences — your inner reality without making the other person responsible for them. An I-message is honest, authentic and congruent. It doesn't judge, blame or interrupt. It never tells the other person what she should think, hope or fear. Since you are saying what you feel, your verbal and nonverbal communication is in harmony. You sound confident and your words and gestures are compatible. Successful use of I-messages requires that you:

- Know what you want and need.

- Take personal responsibility for meeting your preferences.

- Express yourself in an assertive way to the person whose cooperation you need.

- Be willing to listen if the other person becomes defensive.

If you develop a full repertoire of assertive communication, you can choose appropriate and self-fulfilling responses for a variety of situations. All effective assertive communication, however, is characterized by a basic four-part message:

1. Non-judgmental description of the behavior to be changed.

2. Disclosure of the assertor's feelings.

3. Clarification of the concrete and tangible effect of the other person's behavior on the assertor.

4. Description of the behavior that would be more satisfactory.

You'll send more assertive messages when you use this formula: "When you (state the other person's behavior non-judgmentally), I feel (disclose your feelings) because (explain the impact on your life). I prefer (describe what you want)." This way, the four parts of the assertion message are stated as succinctly as possible and are contained in one sentence.

This four-part assertive communication style requires conscientious practice. Others don't know what behavior you want modified. You must communicate what the other person does that frustrates you. This is not easy. People seldom describe behavior accurately enough for listeners to understand how their actions frustrate the speaker. These guidelines will help you develop effective behavior description skills:

• Describe the behavior in specific rather than general terms.

• Limit yourself to behavioral descriptions. Do not draw inferences about the other person's motive, attitudes, character, etc.

- Be objective, not judgmental.

- Be as brief as possible.

- Communicate the real issues.

- Communicate to the right person.

Many will respect your assertive communication style. But be prepared for those who may respond aggressively toward you, using verbal attacks, demands or put-downs. Sadly, many of us are used to the security payoffs non-assertiveness offers. But if you focus on safety, you deny your many strengths and assertive experiences. When you communicate from those strengths, you are most powerful.

Examples of Effective Assertion Messages

Inappropriate Messages:

- "You've ruined another Monday for me."

- "You kids don't appreciate anything that you have."

- "I've really got to go. I've got too much to do to hang on this phone all day."

- "Why am I the only one who does the dinner dishes? I work hard all day too, you know."

Appropriate Messages:

- "When you are late for our appointments I feel frustrated because it throws off my schedule for the rest of the day. I prefer that you schedule our Monday meeting at 9:00 rather than 8:00 to allow you to be on time."

- "When you insist on taking dancing and piano lessons and then refuse to practice either one, I feel unhappy because I have to pay for lessons that you don't fully use. I prefer that you spend money more wisely by choosing only one lesson and following through with the required practice at home."

- "When you call me at work and talk for a long time, I feel tense because I can't get all my work done. I prefer to phone you after my work is done."

- "When you do not put the dishes on the counter, I feel irritated because it makes extra work for me when I am already tired from working all day. I would like everyone to rinse and stack their own place settings on the counter by the dishwasher."

Key Concepts in Chapter 4:

- Human behaviors can be classified as either passive, aggressive, or assertive.

- Assertive behavior is the foundation of effective written and spoken communication.

- Of the three behavior/communication options, assertiveness offers the most rewards for all participants in the communication process.

- Effective assertive communication is characterized by "I" statements.

- The formula for basic assertiveness statements is: "When you (state the feeling or behavior non-judgmentally), I feel (disclose your feelings) because (clarify the effect in your life). I prefer (describe what you want)."

1. Think of a time when you behaved inappropriately with a co-worker. What was responsible for the communication failure? Were you too passive? Too aggressive? How would the four-part formula have affected the outcome?

2. Listen to yourself. Do you send "You" messages? As you become more attuned to your patterns of speech, substitute "I" messages for "You" messages. Write in your journal the effect this has on the people with whom you are speaking.

Reflections

5 IT'S NOT WHAT YOU SAY: IT'S HOW YOU SAY IT

"I have found it enriching to open channels whereby others can communicate their feelings, their private perceptual worlds to me."
—Carl Rogers

How you say something often is more powerful than what you say. How does your nonverbal communication work for you? Your tone of voice and facial expression tell people more than your words. Tone, inflection and facial expressions account for 93 percent of your message. The actual words only account for 7 percent.

You don't need a college education or a big vocabulary to communicate assertively and make yourself understood. It's not what you say, it's how you say it. Your non-verbal communication can either enhance and support what your words say, or detract, or even oppose what you are saying.

The key components of nonverbal communication include:

- **Eye Contact.** The eyes are an important part of nonverbal communication. Speakers who stare off into space or keep their eyes glued to their feet do not inspire much attention or confidence. Some people have a problem with powerful eye contact.

  To communicate more confidence and polish, keep your head up and vary the direction of your gaze. Eye contact emphasizes a point and establishes trust.

In conversation, glance at the other person for a second and then glance away to show you are listening and not just staring. Continuously looking at another person makes him uncomfortable. When speaking, a relaxed and steady gaze, occasionally looking away, shows interest in and respect for the other person and enhances your message. Since we tend to maintain more eye contact with people we think accept and support us, avoiding eye contact indicates low self-esteem. With conscious effort, you can improve your eye contact. Be aware of your eyes as you talk with others and gradually attempt to optimize your eye contact in conversation.

- **Body Posture.** How you carry yourself sends a double nonverbal message. It reveals what you think about yourself and what you think about your listener. Slouching conveys an attitude of indifference to the world. Conversely, if you're rigid and uptight, you communicate anxiety and insecurity. These are two extremes. Try for a happy medium: poised and relaxed, alert but not tense, even when you may not really feel that way. Self-awareness is the secret. When you are aware of how you look, you can obtain the look you want to send to the listener.

Researcher John Malloy found that the most effective stance for both men and women is a straight, almost military spine, head erect, with feet straight and slightly spread apart and arms at the side with fingers lightly cupped. Have you ever noticed the number of people who talk with their bodies turned away from others? People who sit side-by-side often turn only their heads toward one another while talking. Next time you are in this situation, notice how much more personal the conversation gets with a slight turn of your body — say 30 degrees — toward the other person. Relative "power" in an encounter may be emphasized by standing or sitting. If you need to stand up for yourself, do just that — stand up. An erect posture lends additional assertiveness to your message. A slumped, passive stance gives the other person an immediate advantage, as does any tendency on your part to lean or move away.

- **Distance/Physical Contact.** The distance you maintain from other people has a direct impact upon communication. Standing or sitting closely together and touching suggests intimacy in a relationship unless the person is in crowded or very cramped quarters. The typical discomfort most of us feel when there are too many people in an elevator illustrates how coming too close may offend others.

Some people try to dominate others through such territorial moves. Unless you are aware of the significance of such actions, you may unconsciously respond with submissive behavior. If you find yourself in the presence of someone who uses such tactics, hold your ground. Signal your own sense of power in a number of ways, including:

1. Rise, move casually around your office during a conversation.

2. Excuse yourself on the pretext of keeping an appointment.

3. Set up a barrier to screen visitors from your office or desk.

4. Assume the same familiarity with peers by dropping by their offices.

5. Be assertive. Move toward the person.

- **Facial Expressions.** Have you ever seen someone trying to express anger while smiling or laughing? It just doesn't work. Effective communication requires facial expressions that agree with what is being said.

  Let your face say the same thing as your words. Nothing is warmer than a sincere smile, but never force a smile. The listener will know it's phony. If you say something amusing with a smile, your listener will nearly always smile along with you. Even in a serious conversation, the smile is essential. If everything you say is serious, there is no variety, no contrast.

- **Gestures.** Your gestures are as important as your facial expressions. While enthusiastic gesturing is indeed a somewhat culturally related behavior, a relaxed use of gestures adds depth and power to your messages. Uninhibited movement suggests openness, self-confidence and spontaneity on the speaker's part. Effective gestures are either descriptive or emphatic. Descriptive gestures illustrate your point, while emphatic gestures emphasize or underscore specific points in your speech.

- **Vocal Tone, Inflection, Volume.** Your voice is one of your most vital body tools in communication. Words spoken through clenched teeth in anger offer an entirely different message than when the same words are shouted with joy or whispered in fear. A level, well-modulated conversational tone is persuasive without being intimidating. A whispered monotone makes it hard to convince others that you mean business. Consider the three dimensions of your voice:

- **Tone.** Is your tone raspy, whiny, soft, angry? Women tend to have a higher pitched and softer speaking voice than men. A lower pitched voice generally is more effective.

- **Inflection.** Do you emphasize certain syllables as in a question, speak in a monotone or with a sing-song effect? Swings in emotion can be shown with variations in pitch.

- **Volume.** Do you try to gain attention by whispering, or do you overpower others with loudness? Or is it difficult for you to shout even when you want to? Your voice is a powerful tool in self-expression. Control and use it effectively. Practice with a recorder until you achieve a style you like. Allow yourself time for changes to become natural. Use the recorder regularly to check your progress.

- **Fluency.** A smooth flow of speech helps get your point across in any type of conversation. It is not necessary to talk rapidly for an extended period. If your speech is interrupted with long hesitations, your listeners will become bored and sense that you are unsure of yourself. Clear and slow comments are more easily understood and powerful than rapid speech that is erratic.

- **Timing.** In general, spontaneity of expression is the goal. Hesitation diminishes the effectiveness of your message. If a problem arises and you aren't able to express yourself adequately at the time, it is usually worthwhile to find the person later and talk with him about what is on your mind. Effective communication helps keep your relationships open and accurately conveys your feelings.

- **Clothing.** What you wear and how you wear it send powerful signals. Your clothing and accessories are a reflection of your status, who you think you are, and what you want others to think of you. Sometimes this message can be lost or misinterpreted. Clothing revolves around two concerns: how to fit in and how to stand out. The first rule about clothes, accessories and hairstyle is that there are no rules. It's up to you. If you're comfortable with yourself, then you'll be comfortable with whatever you wear. Trying to make yourself look younger or older than you are, or trying to look like someone else are the best ways to make yourself uncomfortable. Avoid extremes unless you're in the business of attracting attention to yourself. Don't be swept away by the latest fashion even if a lot of other people are wearing the same thing. Wear styles and colors that make you look your best.

Please yourself first. But unless you live in a cave, you should recognize that at some times and in some places on some occasions other people's opinion of the way you look and dress are just as important, maybe even more important, than your own preferences. A CEO of a major cosmetic company wears his high school softball cap in the privacy of his office, but not when he meets with the board of directors. A navy suit is appropriate for a business lunch but would be out of place at a backyard barbecue. You don't always want to look like everyone else. Use your imagination and do a little something to set yourself apart. Your clothing is often the first thing people notice about you. When you care enough to present yourself at your best, people will care about you. If you're really not sure what makes you look your best, take the time and effort to find out. Solicit advice from friends and professionals.

The confident communicator develops an effective personal style. He exercises good eye contact and facial expression. He projects an assertive stance. By using appropriate hand and arm gestures, he conveys a feeling of openness and ease. His personal style adds to his confidence. The bottom line is that the powerful communicator develops an assertive aura which frees him from fumbling over every word.

Key Concepts in Chapter 5:

- How you communicate is often more important than what you communicate.

- Nonverbal communication involves several components:

  - Eye contact

  - Body Posture

  - Distance/Physical Contact

  - Facial Expression

  - Gestures

  - Vocal Tone

  - Fluency

  - Timing

  - Dress

- Verbal and nonverbal communication combine to form a personal style that is unique to every communicator.

1. The tape recorder is a valuable tool. Use it to practice by talking about a familiar subject for a few seconds. Listen to yourself, noticing pauses of three seconds or more and space fillers such as "uhh" and "you know." Repeat the same exercise more slowly, if necessary, trying to eliminate any significant pauses. Gradually increase the difficulty by dealing with less familiar topics. Try to be persuasive. Pretend to respond in an argument, or work with a friend to keep a genuine dialogue going.

2. Look in the mirror. What do you see? Do you see a person you would feel confident with? What does your body language say about you? Practice standing and using gestures to bring your message across more directly. Does your body reflect the message you want to give to the world?

3. What do your clothes say about you? Look at your wardrobe. When you shop for clothes, buy things you can mix and match with what you already have. Maybe clothes don't make the man, but they go long way in making a statement about who you are and what you think about yourself.

Reflections

PUBLIC SPEAKING

> "That impromptu speech is most worth listening to which has been carefully prepared in private and tried on a plaster case or an empty chair or any other appreciative object that will keep quiet until the speaker has got his matter and his delivery limbered up so that they will seem impromptu to an audience."
>
> *—Mark Twain*

William Jennings Bryan, flanked by aides, approached the podium at the 1896 Democratic convention to accept his party's nomination for president of the United States and muttered under his breath, "I wish God would strike me dead rather than have to give this speech." This from the man who would be considered one of the greatest American orators of history. In his *Book of Lists,* writer and researcher Irving Wallace reports that the American public's No. 1 fear is speaking before an audience. Stage fright is normal in public speaking. It strikes everyone, famous or not. The difference lies in how we deal with it.

Former Vice President Alden W. Barkley died while giving a speech. He is probably the first person ever to die while speaking in public. Even though your knees knock, your heart races, your palms get sweaty, your mouth feels like cotton and your blood pressure goes up, public speaking is safe. The odds are dramatically in your favor that you will survive the speech.

Toastmasters International says public speaking does not involve eliminating butterflies in your stomach, but simply getting them to fly in formation.

To be a successful public speaker, you must be able to answer the following questions:

1. Who is your audience?

2. What does the audience want most?

3. How can you help get what they want?

The underlying consideration in all public speaking should be time: your time and that of your listeners. First impressions are important. After just a few words, an image is formed in the mind. Get your point across swiftly and succinctly. No matter how interesting your topic, nobody likes to be subjected to a long-winded speaker. Even if this weren't the case, the attention span of the average individual is only about 20 minutes.

To be a successful public speaker:

1. Tell the audience what you are going to say.

2. Say it.

3. Tell them what you said.

The Purpose Is Primary

The first principle of public speaking is to have a clear-cut objective. In *The Wizard of Oz,* Dorothy had an objective, a purpose. It was to get back home to Kansas. She knew what she wanted. Your speech has to have a purpose. What is the point of the speech? Opportunities are wasted when people have unclear or mixed objectives.

The purpose of every speech falls into one of these five categories:

1. To entertain

2. To inform

3. To inspire

4. To convince

5. To persuade

Organize and Arrange

Every speech comes in three parts: the introduction, the body and the conclusion.

1. The introduction is a "hook" to attract interest. Your hook should relate to your listeners as well as your purpose. The introduction can be a question or a statement. It can be dramatic or humorous. If it's a question, it should be answered. Anecdotes and personal experiences make great hooks as long as they appeal to a broad audience. The introduction serves two other purposes. It tells the audience the benefit of listening to the rest of your talk, and it previews what will come.

2. From the introduction, you move to the body of your remarks — the subject. The subject explains and reinforces your objective. The subject must relate to the listeners. What, who, where, when, why and how are all part of your subject. Know your subject and present it as concisely and forcefully as possible.

Remember that in verbal communication there are no second chances for the audience to catch your remarks. Keep your talk simple and easy to understand. Effective speeches contain no more than three central points. Four points is an absolute maximum. More will confuse the audience and waste their time — and yours.

Arrange the main points of your talk into a pattern, such as:

- Time order
- Space order
- Classification order
- Cause and Effect order
- Problem and Solution order

Each of your main points should be supported by interesting and relevant material, such as illustrations, comparisons and contrasts, specific instances, facts and figures, etc. Develop each main point in such a way that the audience will accept it. If they are predisposed to acceptance, your goal is simply to be vivid, impressive and dynamic. The audience doesn't need to be hit over the head with arguments. They are already impressed. They already agree with you.

If the audience is doubtful, be informative. The doubtful audience is looking for information, not memories and quotations. Give them what they're looking for. If the audience is indifferent, use facts. Be compelling and conciliatory. Appeal to their basic wants and needs. Appeal to their open-mindedness and fair play. Do not be argumentative. If the audience is indifferent, impel them by motivation. Show why your idea is important. Make the issue vital to the listener's needs. Give specific comparisons and illustrations.

3. The conclusion of your speech is used as a review. Highlight the key points you want your audience to remember. The listener should leave feeling interested, informed, stimulated, persuaded or convinced after listening to you talk. Your audience should feel rewarded for listening to you. Ask them to act or react to your ideas. A message without a specific request is a wasted opportunity. Move them to action. Call for a specific decision within a specific time frame. A courteous "thank you" is a poor way to end a speech.

While it is still certain that the status, position and occupation of your listeners influences the slant of your remarks, don't talk down to your audience. Don't talk up either. It won't gain you favor. Flattery is transparent. No matter who the person is or what she does, it is far better to talk with her. This is especially true when you want to gain influence. Take into consideration the varying backgrounds of your audience. Whether it is one person or 1000, the same basic principles and strategies of the message apply.

Don't memorize your speech. If you do not memorize it perfectly, you will stumble, or worse, forget. Even if it is well memorized, you have to recall each word as it comes. This preoccupation makes your words sound rehearsed, cold and lifeless instead of spontaneous, warm and earnest.

Don't read your speech, however. When you stand before an audience and fix your eyes on a manuscript, you lose personal contact. This is fatal to your message. Instead, write a rough draft of your speech, and then reduce it to notes on 3" x 5" cards. Rehearse your speech striving for spontaneity, variety and naturalness in your words and movements. Memorize your sequence of ideas. Then rehearse the speech formally five to ten times. This helps you develop a delivery that allows for the right amount of spontaneity. Use the note cards to carry your sequence of major ideas. Do not write the speech out word for word.

Rehearse your speech. You will give the speech standing up. Therefore, rehearse standing up. Rehearse your posture. Rehearse your actions.

If possible, rehearse in a room the same size as the room you will speak in. After you have given several speeches, you will learn how many rehearsals you need for a successful speech.

Successful speaking is a skill just like walking or riding a bicycle. It takes time, training and practice, practice, practice.

Key Concepts in Chapter 6

- Stage fright is normal. The only difference is how you, the speaker, handle it.

- All speeches have one of several purposes: to entertain, inform, inspire, convince or persuade.

- Every speech has three parts: an introduction, a body (the subject) and a conclusion.

- The introduction is designed to attract the listener.

- The body of the speech must be logically organized so the listener will remember what you say.

- Speeches should contain no more than four major points and preferably only three.

- The conclusion should review the main points of the body and challenge the audience to action.

- Rehearse your speech exactly as you wish to deliver it.

- Speak from 3" x 5" note cards, not a manuscript.

1. How do you feel when you are asked to give a speech?
    Nervous? Self-conscious? What is your confidence quotient?
    Before you give a speech, practice what you will say with the
    appropriate body language and gestures you will use. Prac-
    tice until your words, body language and nonverbal commu-
    nications are all in concert.

2. Use your tape recorder. Tape your speech as many times as
    you need to get just the right inflection, tone and emotion into
    your words.

3. Study the techniques of gifted speakers. What do they do that
    you don't? How do they arouse, persuade or motivate?
    Again, use a tape recorder. Tape the speech. Then study it to
    see what makes it work.

Reflections

THE WRITE STYLE

"If a style of writing doesn't come easily to you, then it's probably not coming easily to the reader either. Style must come from who you are, not who you wish you were. Just relax and write as well as you can."

—*Gary Provost*

In all communication, the key to success is knowledge. Write about what you know. If you don't know the topic, you can't write effectively. The more you know something, the easier and more effective your writing. Can you explain the subject in your own words to someone who knows less about it than you do? If not, research more. If so, you are ready to write.

Know your audience. Ask yourself, what do my readers know? What do they need to know? What decisions will be based on this information? Are you writing to increase knowledge? Are you trying to urge action? Know what motivates your readers. Effective writing requires knowledge of your topic, analysis of your reader and a plan to achieve your goal. Most of all, good writing always follows the three Cs: It is Clear, it is Crisp, and it is Concise. The following guidelines will help you follow the three Cs in your writing:

The Systematic Approach

Approach writing systematically. Keep separate tasks separate. Break your writing into small jobs as follows:

1. Research the topic. Study. Read. Talk with informed people. Establish a clear idea of your purpose and an understanding of how the job should be done.

2. Plan. Even a brief sentence outline clarifies your writing goals.

   Before writing ask yourself:

   A. Do I know my subject?

   B. Do I know my reader?

   C. Is this writing necessary?

3. Draft. Rough draft a few pages at a time.

4. Eliminate useless words and sentences. Strive for brevity and concreteness.

5. Type. Get a typed version that is as close to your final draft as possible.

6. Proofread. Proofread once you've arranged your thoughts on paper and edited the unnecessary words and sentences.

Drafting, revising, typing and proofreading are separate jobs that need their own time and attention. Pay attention to one job at a time. How long can you concentrate while writing? Most of us write best if we take a break every twenty minutes. Remember, in writing, activity doesn't always equal productivity. Some of the best writing comes from sitting back and dreaming. Just as children need rules and structure to be happy, so do writers. Be kind to yourself. Establish specific guidelines for tackling a writing project. Set reasonable deadlines to do a good job.

Learn from Mistakes

Learn why you're making mistakes. Nearly every example of poor writing fits under one or more of the following six stumbling blocks. The writer:

1. Didn't know the subject.

2. Didn't know the audience.

3. Didn't start early enough.

4. Needs a refresher course in grammar.

5. Was trying to impress someone.

6. Was trying to deceive.

If you can correct these fundamental problems, you've taken a giant step to becoming a better writer.

Thought Patterns

Establish a thought pattern for your writing. Whatever the pattern, it must include:

1. Information and details about why you are writing.

2. Information and details about the subject.

3. Information and details that support your statements.

4. Remedies, solutions, suggestions, ideas, plans, actions already taken. Remember to include a description of the benefits that result from adopting your suggestions.

5. When you've completed your background research, how do you begin writing? There are several ways to arrange the information:

   A. Chronologically with points arranged in the order they happened or should happen.

   B. In order of importance, from the most to the least important.

   C. Showing cause and effect stating what was done and what resulted.

   D. From general to specific. Start with broad statements followed by the advantages and reasons.

   E. Pros and cons. Give reasons for and against something. This is often best when the decision isn't yours to make, and you want your supervisor to be able to weigh all the facts before making a decision.

Reflect Personal Style

Make your writing reflect your personal style. A personal tone makes even the driest subject interesting. To achieve conversational tone, write as if you are talking to the reader. You can achieve this if you:

1. Drop stiff, formal phrases. Most business people prefer a casual, direct style to the formality of our grandparents' days. Avoid archaic words and phrases like "institutionalize" and "Upon receipt of your order, our engineering department will be instructed to begin assembly." Instead try, "Our engineers will assemble your unit when the order arrives."

2. Use contractions where they sound right to you. Contractions add a little human touch in your writing, if used sparingly.

3. Downplay the number of personal pronouns in your writing. Don't overuse "I," " you," "we," "he," "she," "mine," "yours," etc. Too many of these weaken your message. An occasional pronoun is fine. But when in doubt, throw it out.

Paragraph Power

Practice Paragraph Power. Paragraphs consist of three to five sentences. For significant improvement in your writing skills, focus on the topic sentence and keep the supporting sentences in the paragraph relevant.

The topic sentence generally belongs at the beginning of the paragraph. It is the sentence that tells the reader the main focus of the paragraph. You can increase the dramatic effect of the paragraph if you save the topic sentence till the end. But beware — you may lose your reader. Remember, there are differences between business writing and writing a novel.

Make each subsequent sentence count. Make sure it adds to or explains what you say in your topic sentence. This achieves relevance.

Transitions are also important. Transitions tie your paragraphs together, and establish a sense of unity and flow to your writing. When you want transition between paragraphs:

1. Use a word or words in the first sentence of a new paragraph that are in the last line of the previous paragraph.

2. Use a word at the beginning of a paragraph that makes sense only when read in relation to the previous paragraph. Transition words and phrases to use at the beginning of a new paragraph include *nevertheless, later, of course, for example, therefore, because of this, in the meantime, needless to say, etc.*

3. Use a paragraph heading to announce what the next paragraph is about.

Sentence Savvy

Just as paragraphs can be punched up, so can sentences. If your writing is failing, try one of these formulas for better sentences.

1. Look at 150 words in your writing. Count the number of one-syllable words. Divide that number by 10 and subtract the result from 20. The number you get is the number of years of school your readers need to read your writing easily. The more challenging the subject is, the simpler your writing should be. *The New York Times* and *The Wall Street Journal* are written for grades eight through 12. The editors know their readers want business information fast and uncomplicated. Your readers want the same.

2. Eliminate prefixes such as pre-, anti-, and multi- as well as suffixes such as -ability, -tion, and -ism.

3. Your sentences should average 15 to 22 words. None of them should be longer than 40 words. This is a guideline often used by newspapers. Long sentences slow comprehension because they contain many elements that have to be related to one another.

4. Get rid of anemic introductory phrases such as, "there is," "there are," "it appears," "it would seem that." These phrases say nothing, and because they are at the beginning of a sentence, what comes after them often seems lifeless. Avoid unnecessary prepositions like, *on, up beside, before, behind, between, against, for, off, despite, by, in, into, among, across, toward, without, under, onto.*

5. Break long sentences into two shorter sentences. Vary sentence structure. Create a variety of sentences; long and short, simple and complex, active and passive. Use these patterns to create an easy flow to your writing. Make your sentences interlock like pieces of a jigsaw puzzle.

For additional help with your writing, pick up a copy of Robert Iles' *Techniques to Improve Your Writing Skills.* This brief, direct manual is packed with tips to improve your writing. Or, pick up any of Gary Provost's books on writing. Before long writing will come easily for you.

Key Concepts in Chapter 7

- Effective writing requires a knowledge of the subject, an analysis of the reader and a plan.

- Evaluate why you are writing. What is the purpose?

- Learn from your mistakes. Are you getting tripped by one of the six stumbling blocks?

- Determine a pattern for your writing.

- Express a personal style. Convey your personality as well as your thoughts and ideas.

- Evaluate paragraphs for topic sentence, relevance, unity and transitions. Refine your sentences.

1. Remember the three Cs of good writing. Is your writing Clear, Crisp and Concise? Do you use active verbs? Instead of "The instructions are enclosed," try "I have enclosed the instructions." As you read newspapers and magazine, look for dull, lifeless writing. How would you wake it up?

2. Study your favorite authors. What makes their writing work? How does King or Ludlam make you jump? Read your favorite passages to see what gives their writing impact.

3. Write and rewrite. As with any skill, the more you practice, the more proficient you become.

Reflections

COMPLIMENTS AND CRITICISM

"Can I be strong enough as a person to be separate from the other? Can I be a sturdy respecter of my own feelings, my own needs, as well as his?"

—Carl Rogers

At first glance, a compliment appears easier to receive than criticism or rejection. However, each can be charged with emotional pleasure. You can learn to successfully handle them all.

Compliments

Charlotte gave a brilliant performance during her violin concert and she knew it. The months of hard work and long hours of practice clearly showed. As her friends and colleagues complimented her achievement during the next several days, Charlotte found herself blushing and stammering. She was frustrated with her reaction. Knowing the compliments were genuinely deserved did nothing to calm her fear that they might not really be genuine on the part of those assuring her of her expertise.

When someone pays you a compliment, how do you react? Do you look for the other person's motive? Do you shrug it off with tag lines like "Oh, it was nothing?" or "It had to be done anyway?" The confident communicator accepts the compliment as a frank expression of appreciation.

53

Some people suspect compliments are insincere. While not all compliments are genuine, you should assume the best. Say "Thank you" and take the compliment at face value. If you feel uncomfortable receiving a compliment because you feel obligated to compliment the other person, understand that it is not necessary to reciprocate. However, it is important to acknowledge what the other person has said to you. You can do this verbally or nonverbally with a smile or a nod of recognition.

In addition to acknowledging the compliment verbally by saying "Thank you," you might want to indicate how you feel about what was said. Try adding, "I really appreciate that you notice my efforts," or "I'm glad you think so," or "Thanks for letting me know that." Avoid making excuses for the compliment by saying something like, "You caught me on a good day." To discount the compliment with an irrelevant verbal reply is a serious blow to your verbal communication power. Believe in yourself. Accept the compliment. You are a valuable person capable of doing something worthy of appreciation and admiration.

Compliments make us feel good about ourselves. If you can't get a compliment anywhere, give yourself one. We become who we think we are. Avoid the tendency to criticize yourself. Believe in your talents and abilities. Young and old, we all have days that we say things to ourselves like:

1. "Nobody loves me."

2. "People are just plain rotten."

3. "Nobody listens to me."

4. "I am such a jerk."

Whenever you catch yourself talking to yourself this way, turn it around and concentrate on positive labels. Just as children believe what they are told, so do we come to believe the messages we give ourselves. Turn negative statements like the above into positive thoughts by changing the negative to positive:

1. "People respect me."

2. "People usually mean well."

3. "People listen to what I say."

4. "I am powerful when I communicate assertively."

Continual self-doubt and criticism can become a downward spiral. Stop imagining the worst and consider ways to create a complimentary attitude.

Criticism

Joseph lives in constant fear of losing his new job. Although he is well qualified for his work in engineering, the criticisms he received the first couple of weeks in his position as he "learned the ropes" left him feeling insecure. He spends a lot of mental energy anticipating the next criticism by his boss and wondering how to avoid it.

We don't experience inhibition just when we give and receive compliments. We feel the same inhibition when we give and receive criticism. Underlying the fear of giving and accepting criticism is the fear of rejection. When your self-esteem is low, it doesn't take much to paralyze you with anxiety and fear at the moment of making or receiving critical remarks. Likewise, as your confidence level climbs higher with your increasing assertiveness, your ability to objectively evaluate criticism becomes stronger and clearer.

The element of surprise is one of the things that make criticism hard to take. Criticism that is least expected usually hurts the most. To overcome the fear of criticism, it is important to set up a step-by-step process that gradually desensitizes you to critical remarks whether they are anticipated or unexpected.

Take a good look at yourself. The assertive person is careful not to over-prepare or feel he must be constantly on guard. Be realistic. Know your strengths and work on your weaknesses.   Prepare for three possible types of criticism:

1. Unrealistic criticism.

2. Put-down criticism.

3. Valid criticism.

Unrealistic criticism is ridiculous to the point of being opposite of the truth. The put-down may have an element of truth but is said in such a way as to patronize or insult rather than be productive. Valid criticism is realistic and stated in a straightforward, assertive manner.

Put-Downs

Put-downs come in all shapes and sizes. They may be direct or indirect. From time to time, we all encounter put-downs and criticism. By using these communication techniques, you will be able to keep your head high:

1. Allow the emotion to dissipate.

2. Admit when you are wrong, even if you have been insulted.

3. Acknowledge the other person's feelings about the situation.

4. Assert yourself in confronting the other person's reactions to you.

5. Draw the encounter to an end.

Here's how this works: Recently Jake's friend Susan dropped in to go to lunch with him. On his way out of the office, the phone rang. Jake stopped at Veronica's desk to answer the phone. Unable to find a pen and paper on the desk to leave a message, he searched the desk drawer. In the middle of his search, Veronica returned to her desk. Seeing Jake go through her desk, she blew up. She shouted, "You jerk! You've got no business rummaging through my things. Get out of here!" Jake was stunned, angry and embarrassed in front of his friend. He kept his cool, though.

When Veronica finished, Jake said, "I apologize for moving the papers on your desk and opening the drawer to search for a pen. Obviously, you are upset. Your phone rang as I was on my way to lunch. I thought the call might be important and picked it up for you. There was no pen and paper on the desk to write you a note. I don't like being yelled at for doing you a favor. Next time, please check the situation out before you jump on me." Still angry, but with his cool in place, Jake and Susan proceeded out the door to lunch.

Indirect put-downs are trickier to handle. Not only do you have to deal with the emotion of the conflict, but you have to teach the other person to deal with you directly. For example, you wear your favorite sweater to your mother's house and she says, "I just love that on you. Only you can get away with wearing a color like that." How do you respond? Was it a compliment or a put-down? The strategy for handling situations like this is to seek more information. Ask for specifics. "What do you mean, Mom? Is this an unusual color? Does that mean you like it, Mom?" Your next response depends on the answers to these questions. By doing this, you are modeling effective communication. If your mother doubts the beauty of your orange and black sweater, that's okay. "You are right, Mom. Different strokes for different folks. I like this sweater. It suits my mood today." Don't let other people's opinions intentionally or unintentionally deflate your balloon.

Rejection

Nobody likes rejection, but the confident, assertive communicator knows that it is both natural and unavoidable. Rejection occurs when someone says, "no" to your idea, request or action. Some people need the approval of other people. They are vulnerable when told "no." The assertive person accepts "no" as a denial in a specific situation and doesn't think she is rejected as a person.

Communication is the expression of another's perception. "No" is not a rejection of you. It is the rejection of an idea. Don't take it personally. This only complicates your ability to communicate and decreases your effectiveness and understanding of the situation. Don't give up on people. While you might meet some dishonest manipulators who say, "no" and mean it as a direct rejection of you, most want the same things from communication as you do.

No one likes to be talked down to. Nobody likes rejection. But honest and straightforward clarification of criticism or rejection helps you to resolve the conflict. Concentrate on remaining objective and not giving in to your emotions.

Conflict caused by criticism and rejection can be resolved if you put on your "assertive" face. Clarify the situation with yourself and the other involved. Don't store up bad feelings of rejection and anger only to have them resurface at a later time. Clear the air. Express your feelings. Accept the feelings and information of the other person. Then move on.

Key Concepts in Chapter 8

- To successfully deal with compliments, criticism and rejection, keep your head when under pressure.

- You are a valuable person who will receive both compliments and criticism.

- In conflict situations, deal with the emotion first. Diffuse the emotions, so you can analytically look at the information from the other person's perspective.

- Even though it's difficult, don't take emotion-laded statements personally.

- Allow yourself to be assertive, clarify the situation and express your feelings without dwelling on them.

1. Catch your reflection in the mirror without changing your facial expression. What do you see? A happy, confident sort of person? Or a sour, unpleasant person? Look in the mirror again. Smile at the reflection you see. Notice how much younger you look. A smile is an instant face-lift. Make an effort to reveal the pleasant side of you. As Dale Carnegie said, "No one argues with a smile."

2. Believe in your talents. Believe in your abilities. Believe in yourself. We become what we think of ourselves. Surround yourself with positive thoughts about yourself. In the beginning this takes practice. Recent research shows that holding ourselves in positive regard nurtures us and helps us grow into the persons we want to be. Take the time to praise yourself for a job well done or new skills you add to your communication behavior.

3. When someone criticizes you, do you feel devastated? Incompetent? Less than you are? Practice asking yourself, is the criticism unrealistic? Is it a put-down? Could it be valid? Don't take all criticism the same way. Handle the criticism for what it is. Always remember that you are a valuable person regardless of others' approval.

4. How do you criticize others? Is the criticism valid? Is it a put-down? Or is it unrealistic? Put yourself in the other person's shoes? How does your own criticism feel? If you wouldn't want your words said to you, don't say them to somebody else.

Reflections

SUCCESSFUL PROBLEM-SOLVING

" ... I have come to feel that the more I can keep relationships free of judgment and evaluation, the more this will permit the other person to reach the point where he recognizes that the focus of evaluation, the center of responsibility, lies within himself."

—Carl Rogers

History teaches us that conflict is dangerous unless it is controlled by regulations. When nations go to war, there are some agreed-upon rules of conduct. When high-school girls play basketball, they are protected from certain types of violence by the rules that govern the sport. And yet the most important conflicts of our lives are unregulated. When parents and teen-agers, co-workers and long-time friends argue, rarely are there agreed-upon rules to protect them and their relationships. This chapter encourages assertive communication and the expression of feelings without permitting a verbal free-for-all to block creative resolution of conflict and destroys relationships. Problem-solving is a process that generates constructive "fights" in a systematic, non-injurious, growth-producing manner.

Whenever feelings and emotions are unusually high, it is important to alleviate the emotional aspects of conflict at the outset. Anger, distrust, scorn, fear, rejection and defensiveness — these emotions collide head-on with the real issues of the conflict, such as opposing needs, disagreements over policies and practices, and differing concepts of roles and resources. Only when the emotional aspects of the conflict have been resolved can the parties proceed to the next stage, the rational and creative examination of the actual issues that divide them.

Collaborative Problem-Solving

Skill in listening, assertion and conflict resolution are required in collaborative problem-solving. In addition, you need to understand what Bolton defines as the Collaborative Problem-Solving Method. Here are the six steps of Bolton's process:

1. Define the problem.

2. Brainstorm possible solutions.

3. Select the solution that best satisfies both parties.

4. Define how the decision will be implemented.

5. Implement the plan.

6. Evaluate the process and the solution.

Let's explore each step briefly.

1. *Define the problem/Assert your needs.* Listen reflectively until you understand the other person's needs. Include those needs in a short summary of the problem. Except for very simple and difficult problems, allow five to 20 minutes for this step. As Grandma said, "A problem well defined is half solved."

2. *Brainstorm possible solutions.* Brainstorming is the rapid listing of possible solutions without any clarification, evaluation or judgment. Brainstorming focuses on quantity, not quality. It is essential for you not to come into a problem-solving session with the attitude that there is only one adequate solution to the conflict.

3. *Select a mutually satisfying solution.* Suggest more than one solution to the problem, then ask your opponent which of the proposed alternatives he favors to solve the problem. State which alternatives look best to you. See which choices coincide. Then jointly decide on one or more of the alternatives. Be sure your opponent is satisfied with the solution. Once you have agreed to a solution, it is important to try to foresee the possible consequences of the solution.

4. *Plan who will do what to implement the solution.* Sometimes the solution is such an accomplishment that implementation is overlooked and taken for granted. The parties involved need to decide who will do what, where and by when. If necessary, write down your agreement, date it and sign it.

5. *Implement the plan.* The first four points in the problem-solving process are generally resolved during your first discussion. Now it is time to act. Be sure to follow through and do what you promised. If the implementation falls short for whatever reason, it may require an assertive message and reflective listening to avoid subsequent conflict.

6. *Evaluate the process and the solution.* It is important for the parties involved to question the collaborative process. Helpful points to consider in your evaluation include:

   A. What did each person like about the process?

   B. What did each person like least about the process?

   C. What can each party do better next time?

Sidestep Stumbling Blocks

When the collaborative approach to problem-solving fails, it is usually one of the following stumbling blocks that derails the process:

1. *Emotions.* Emotions must be tempered to a tolerable level for the collaborative approach to function effectively.

2. *Unclear Definitions.* Some people do not listen long enough, openly enough or efficiently enough to understand the other person's needs. Many fail to accurately define their own needs through a clearly stated assertion. Use your communication skills to help others define their needs — and understand yours.

3. *Derailed Brainstorming.* Many people fail to stick to the meat and potatoes of brainstorming. Some are wordy and often cannot refrain from adding their opinions and comments. Again, through assertive communication keep brainstorming on track.

4. *Pinpointing Details.* Some people feel that specifying all the details of an agreement implies a lack of trust in the other individual. Others are simply impatient and refuse to take the time to spell out the specifics. Insist upon having your need to communicate met.

5. *Follow-through.* Time is the critical factor here. Many well-intentioned people fail to follow through with their part of the solution. Realize that lack of follow-through doesn't necessarily imply that they don't care about you and the agreement — it may simply mean they lack the skills to follow through.

Benefits of Collaboration

Collaborative problem-solving is mutual affirmation of individual worth. By opting for the collaborative approach, you are saying to the other person that his needs are important to you and that yours are equally valuable. You show respect for his ability to think creatively and regard for his initiative in facing common problems. Using the process implies that both parties have the power to change their behaviors in ways that will improve their relationship. The evaluation act indicates mutual humanity, that people can err and improve. The desire to improve the relationship underscores your respect for the other individual and the value you place on your relationship.

Key Concepts in Chapter 9:

- Collaborative problem-solving is a technique to solve the fundamental cause of a conflict after the emotions of the situation have been defused.

- Collaborative problem-solving is a six-step process.

    1. Define the problem.

    2. List the possible solutions.

    3. Select the mutually satisfying solution.

    4. Plan how to implement the solution.

    5. Implement the plan.

    6. Evaluate the problem-solving process.

- Collaborative problem-solving indicates mutual respect for the parties involved.

- Collaborative problem-solving may take longer, but it is more effective in resolving conflicts permanently.

1. Reflect on your problem-solving techniques. How do you go about solving a problem? Do you jump right in? Or, do you first define the problem with careful reflective listening? Practice the art of waiting until you have all the pieces of the problem. Information is a valuable problem-solving tool.

2. Does your brainstorming identify numerous possible options for a solution? Remember, brainstorming is just the throwing out of ideas for possible explorations while reserving judgment.

3. Are you comfortable with the solution? Is the other person comfortable with the solution? Unless both parties are comfortable, the problem is not solved but merely put on hold. Remember, it may take longer to problem solve with Bolton's method, but the effects are long-lasting.

Reflections

EFFECTIVE CONFLICT COMMUNICATION

"Conflict is an expressed struggle in which two or more interdependent parties are experiencing strong emotion resulting from a perceived difference in needs or values."

—John W. Lawyer

Through a clerical error, two Little League teams were scheduled to practice on the same ballfield at the same time. As the coaches of the Bears and the Eagles shouted and threatened each other, the team members became increasingly embarrassed for them. Some of the kids drifted off. Others ran home. By the time the leadership had hashed things out, there weren't enough players left for a decent practice session for either team.

We shout at each other, take unrelenting "positions," make dogmatic assertions, create facts, and in general, try to "win" our arguments whenever we feel victimized by a process we are unable to control.

James Madison, renowned statesman and former President once wrote, "The most common and durable source of faction has been the various and unequal distribution of property. Central to our everyday squabbles is the fact that we are human ... not gods. No one can rise completely above the selfishness and misrepresentations that strain and even break relationships."

Whether you are a head of state or a Little League coach, conflict is an unavoidable fact of life. At its worst, conflict is destructive. Yet, conflict can offer some important benefits. It can encourage personal and intellectual growth. It can spur technological development, and help create and review our social, religious, political and business organizations. Conflict can be healthy to the development of an institution. It even can be healthy to the development of an individual. Harvard researcher Erick Erickson says the failure to achieve intimacy is the result of an inability to engage in controversy and useful combat. Research also shows that families who openly express dissension and disagreement tended to raise children who have that priceless quality — high self-esteem. But the benefits of conflict only come with being able to handle it well.

The skilled communicator knows how to deal with conflict. Her goal is not to do away with conflict — her goal is to handle it in such a way that it brings about growth and constructive solutions. She knows that different opinions, opposing values, and conflict of desires are the stuff of daily living.

Conflict Resolution Styles

We all have our own ways of dealing with conflict, our own styles of handling difficult situations. How do you manage conflict to minimize risks and maximize benefits? How can you handle conflict in a way that increases your growth potential? The following lists ways we deal with conflict in a small group. Which one of these most closely resembles the way you handle the conflict in your life?

- *The Avoider.* Some people strive for neutrality because they are uncomfortable with anger in any form. Sometimes their avoidance creates conflict or makes a heated situation worse.

- *The Accommodator.* The Accommodator tries to make everyone happy. This person's objective is superficial harmony, not necessarily an equitable resolution of the conflict.

- *The Compromiser.* The Compromiser offers a solution which, at first glance, appears to resolve conflict. However, both sides are left unsatisfied because both give up something they wanted.

- *The Competitor.* For the Competitor, conflict is a sport. There will be a winner and a loser. What gets this person's attention? Power. *[Collaboration]*

- *The Negotiator.* This person seeks consensus and works tirelessly to get it.

Avoidance can be of benefit to you if you are not part of the problem or part of the solution. It is not always your responsibility to "fix" every conflict that arises in your home or workplace.

Accommodation is preferred when the issues are minor or when the relationship would be irreparably damaged because tempers are too hot. Here the solution is only temporary.

Compromise works best when time is short and both parties benefit. But it's a less than perfect situation because everyone loses something.

The competitive approach is best when all parties recognize the power relationship between themselves and know that action is imperative. Like the others, this is merely a temporary answer. This conflict returns, perhaps in a more powerful form.

Negotiation works best when all parties have problem-solving skills. Negotiators work to find methods satisfactory to both parties while keeping goals and values intact. This is the best remedy for communication breakdown.

Defusing Conflict

The first goal in resolving conflict is to deal constructively with the emotions involved. Remember to:

1. Treat the other person with respect.

2. Listen until you "experience the other side."

3. State your views, needs and feelings.

Ironically, while talking may trigger conflict, it is also the only means of resolving conflict. Talking must focus on four simple steps.

1. Define the problem by saying, "I hear ..."

2. Look for agreement by saying, "I agree ..."

3. Understand feelings. "I understand ..."

4. State views calmly. "I think ..."

Some people plunge head first into conflict without determining if their timing is right to resolve the situation. Some forget to set the terms for the confrontations. Others jump into a conflict without knowing if the other person consents to the terms. Check it out. Does each party have sufficient emotional energy to discuss the conflict? Who should be there? When is the best time? Where is the best place?

Conflict resolution directly impacts the emotionality of an interaction. Using the four simple steps encourages the genuine and direct expression of feelings by one person at a time. When feelings are expressed, heard and acknowledged, they are transient. When they are not expressed, heard or acknowledged, they fester. This approach can rapidly defuse emotions so differences can be discussed more productively.

While all of these issues are significant, the most important part of preparation is to refrain from making a surprise attack on the other person. The conflict that begins with mutual consent and agreed-upon conditions (including the use of the conflict resolution method) is off to an effective outcome.

Evaluating the Conflict

Just as important as choosing your approach to conflict resolution is learning valuable lessons from the conflict. Here are questions to help you learn from your conflicts.

1. What have I learned from this experience?

2. Can I learn what I tend to be over-sensitive about or about sensitivities?

3. How well did I use the conflict resolution process: respect, listening, stating my view?

4. How badly was I hurt?

5. How badly was my opponent hurt?

6. How valuable was this conflict for letting off steam?

7. How useful was it in revealing new information about myself, my opponent and the issue in contention?

8. Did either of us change our opinions?

9. What did I learn about my own and my opponent's conflict style, strategy and weapons?

10. What do I want to do differently next time?

11. What do I wish my opponent would do differently next time?

This method promotes understanding and change. No one has the whole truth. I may adopt new ideas and methods or incorporate part of my opponent's approach. Conversely, my opponent may adopt mine. This method improves communication in stressful times. A third alternative also exists. Two parties may jointly develop a creative solution to the substantive issues of the conflict.

The greatest value of this system is that effective handling of conflict deepens and enriches relationships. Relationships falter because individuals don't know how to handle differences. To ignore the differences and use inadequate methods to deal with conflict means you resign yourself to superficial relationships. To fight over differences using inadequate methods causes heartache and blows conflicts out of proportion.

Use this method alone or in agreement with the other person. Or, have it facilitated by a neutral third party. Remember, the best human relationships exist on the other side of the conflict. To get over the emotional hurdle of conflict and resolve substantive issues that triggered the disagreement, work with the conflict resolution to defuse emotions. Once this is accomplished, you are ready to solve the problems that ignited the original conflict.

Key Concepts in Chapter 10:

- There are as many different causes of conflict as there are people.

- When handled constructively, conflict offers advantages for participants.

- There are five basic approaches to conflict:

  1. Avoidance

  2. Accommodation

  3. Compromise

  4. Competition

  5. Negotiation

- There are appropriate times for using each of these conflict strategies.

- The basic purpose of conflict resolution is to defuse emotional roadblocks that stop participants from solving the substantive issues of their dispute.

1. Think of a recent conflict experience in your personal life. Who was there? Who originated the conflict? What did you do? What was the response? What happened? How did you feel? What style did you use? How appropriate was it to the situation? As you reflect on the experience, what would you do the same? What would you do different?

2. Think of a recent conflict experience in your professional life. Who was there? Who originated the conflict? What did you do? What was the response? What happened? How did you feel? What style did you use? How appropriate was it to the situation? As you reflect on the experience, what you do the same? What would you do differently?

Reflections

WHAT IS YOUR CHARISMA QUOTIENT?

"charisma - 1.a. The power or quality of winning the devotion of large numbers of people. b. Great personal magnetism: CHARM. 2. A divinely inspired gift or power, as the ability to perform miracles."

—Webster's II New Riverside Dictionary

When you think of people who have charisma, whom do you think of? Billy Graham? John F. Kennedy? Author and psychologist, Suzette Haden-Elgin says that charisma is the "mysterious, irresistible, almost magical ability to make others believe you and want to do anything you ask of them." Charisma makes people want to trust us. It is a valuable tool, not only in speaking, selling and advertising, but also as a useful addition to your people skills. What if you had the power to lead and persuade people?

People tend to use one of the five sensory modes. Learn which sensory mode the person you are speaking with is in and speak in the same mode. For example, a person speaking in the sight sensory mode will say things like, "I see what you mean," or "That looks good to me." If he is in a hearing mode, he might say things like, "I hear what you're trying to say," or "That sounds fine to me." If he is in a touch mode, he might say something like, "That doesn't feel right to me," or "I can't put my finger on the problem." A person in the smell mode says things like, "I smell a rat," or "Something is fishy." A person in the taste mode says things like, "It leaves a bad taste in my mouth," or "I want it so bad, I can taste it."

Respond in the same mode. If someone says, "This doesn't look right to me," comment with, "I see what you mean," not "I hear what you're saying." Or if someone says, "How does this look?" I reply with "It shows judgment on your part," not "It touches my discerning qualities."

Done properly, mode matching allows the other person to feel accepted, listened to and understood. It creates a connecting energy between you and others.

The verbs people use also help you determine sensory modes and communicate in them without being repetitive. Listen to the verbs people use and match them to the sensory modes. People who use verbs like *see, look,* and *show* prefer the sight sensory mode. *Hear, listen* and *sounds like* indicate a person's preference for the hearing sensory mode, while *touch, feel* and *grip* show an inclination for the touch mode. *Taste, gobble* and *makes me sick* indicate the taste mode. Listen for these verbs and adjust your own to match the other person's.

Charismatic speech is balanced speech. This balance creates a rhythm people respond to positively. When you listen to a charismatic person notice that his speech sounds effortless. We catch on to the speech pattern and know what to expect. There are no surprises. This manner of speaking is known linguistically as *parallelism.* The easiest way to work toward a balanced speech is to be sure that whenever there is more than one of anything, the same language form is used.

There is affirmative parallelism and negative parallelism as in "I will stay, and I will work," and "I will neither stay nor work." There is an order in parallelism and a lack of distraction that allows the listener to relax and allow the rhythm of the communication to bring home the words. A relaxed listener is a more approachable. Tone is equally important. Remember, how you say something affects what others hear. Listen to yourself with an ear toward hearing yourself as others hear you.

Key Concepts in Chapter 11

- People tend to speak in one of the five sensory modes.

- Learn which sensory mode the person with whom you are speaking is in and try to speak in the same mode.

- Parallelism is balanced speech that creates a rhythm to which people tend to give a positive response.

- There is affirmative parallelism and negative parallelism.

- Parallelism allows the listener to relax. A relaxed listener is a more approachable listener.

1. Match verbs from your own listening practices and add them to the following examples to increase your charisma quotient.

Mode	Verb
Sight	see, look, observe, be obvious, be clear
Hearing	hear, listen, pay attention to, sounds like
Touch	touch, feel, grasp, handle, grip
Smell	smell, odor, foul stench, reeks
Taste	taste, gobble, make you sick, be on the tip of your tongue

2. See if you can choose the sentence in each of the following that illustrates parallelism.

    A. "I'm hurt, I'm upset and I'm annoyed," or "I'm hurt and you made me upset, and I'm annoyed too."

    B. "If you're nervous, say so. If you're afraid tell me, and if you're mixed up, try to figure out why." Or, "Tell me whether or not you're nervous," and, "If I don't know if you're mixed up, how can I help you if you haven't even tried to figure it out?"

The correct choice in both sets of sentences is the first pattern.

Reflections

THE GLOBAL WATER COOLER

"You better know that an electronic mail address on the Net is way cooler than a phone number ... the Internet is one more thing. It's the trendiest non-place in the universe."

—*Popular Science*

Communications have exploded in this Information Age. Thousands of people communicate each day by connecting to the Information Superhighway and the number grows daily. Dial in, enter your password and connect to the Internet. Send and receive documents of any nature instantaneously on your fax machine. Leave a message for 42 sales-people on voice mail without having to track them down. Hold a conference call on the world's biggest party line. The whole planet is at your fingertips. It is in your telephone.

Surfing "The Net"

What and where is the Internet? It is not a place. The Internet is a communications network that links computers all around the world via modems. Companies buy and sell on the Internet. They bounce market ideas off potential customers before full launches. They send documents from one place to another in minutes and conduct job interviews in real time.

Consider, if you will, the virtual office. IBM in New Jersey cut the number of offices down from 850 to 150 by putting many of their sales and sales support people on the road and providing them with laptop computers and cellular phones. The company saved $70 million dollars.

Bristol-Meyers Squibb provided each of its 2,000 salespeople with a laptop and product catalogs on CD-ROM, and experienced a rise in productivity. Richard Nolan, a business administration professor at the Harvard Business School says, "My guess is that within three years, the virtual office will no longer be regarded as an experiment. It will be mainstream."

The future of communications is now. If cyberspace intimidates you, if the Internet dismays you, if the World Wide Web makes your skin crawl, relax. You don't need to learn everything overnight. Start with the basics and join the ranks of the computer-friendly as e-mail, faxing and voice mail replace air mail, messenger services and answering machines.

Enjoying E-mail

E-mail is electronic mail. For speed of delivery, e-mail is the quickest way to go. Correspondence gets from one place to another in a matter of minutes. Once you decide to connect to the Internet, your connection provides you with e-mail services and an e-mail address which will look something like this:

> nickname@someplace.com

Your e-mail address means something. @ simply means at, and com indicates the domain, in this case, a company. Other domains are:

1. edu — educational institution; for example, nickname@nyu.edu for someone at New York University.

2. gov — government site; for example, nickname@nasa.gov for someone at NASA.

3. mil — military site; for example, nickname@af.mil for someone in the Air Force.

4. net — network site, for providers and hosts, for example: nickname@li.net for someone at Long Island Net.

5. org — organization sites that do not fit the other classification; for example, nickname@AAG.org. for someone at the Association of American Geographers.

You will also receive an STMP or Simple Mail Protocol server which allows you to send and receive mail. Once you familiarize yourself with the Internet, you will choose the e-mail program that is best suited to your own needs.

Most programs are activated with a click of your mail icon. This click brings you into your mailbox. With another click, you can open and read your mail. Or, click a different menu option and print out the hard copy. You can forward the mail to as many people as you want anywhere in the world, just by typing their e-mail addresses and clicking another icon. You can send carbon copies that list the names of all the people you are sending it to, or you can send them without the list. You can attach minutes of Friday's meeting or a copy of last year's budget report. You can attach any file that is in your computer.

Suppose you need to rent a car. You can do this through your e-mail. Just fill out an electronic form and e-mail it to a special address. From there it is sent though the correct signature chain to get approval. The end product of this sequence is a rental car order. Or suppose your company is in the market to buy a thousand personal computers. Send your request via e-mail to contractors who, in turn, can send engagement letters back to you stating their terms. While it is not a legal contract, everything can be spelled out in the most efficient, time-saving way.

More and more businesses rely on e-mail for in-house correspondence as well as outside dealings. The savings in time and postage alone offer a big advantage over federal mail.

Matter of Fax

Most companies today, large or small, have a fax machine. This allows them to send facsimiles of any document. The major advantage of faxing over sending an e-mail is you can send a fax to a fax machine, but you have to send e-mail to a computer. With a fax machine, you can send anything you have on paper including diagrams and legal documents. This way, you do not have to have the items scanned into your computer.

Imagine you are a sports writer in California dealing with a newspaper in New York. You just covered a baseball game between the California Angels and the Cleveland Indians. The story is scheduled for the next day's issue. What is a quick way to get your story to the newspaper? Fax it!

Most computers today come with a fax modem that connects you to a phone line. This allows you to send any file in your word processing program directly to another computer. Create your document in your word processing program just as you want it to be sent to the newspaper. (Don't forget to save a copy for yourself.) With most programs, this is as easy as going to your menu and clicking on your printer selection choice. Change the information in this box from your printer to your fax program. Proceed as you would if you were printing out your document on your printer. When you instruct your computer to Print, your word processing program thinks it is printing the document. But it is sending it to your fax program, where it stays, until you are ready to send the fax.

You can attach memos, include cover sheets and even sign your fax. To include your signature, you need to have it scanned and put into a graphics file. Then, just enter the fax number of the newspaper and click on Send. The fax program even displays the status of your fax as it is being sent and tells you when it has reached the other computer.

Voice Mail: The New Pony Express

Consider the speed and efficiency of e-mail. Voice mail has many of the same advantages without the need for everyone to have a computer. Voice mail supplants the answering machine. Imagine being able to send a message to anyone in the world wherever they are that they can pick up when they get to the nearest phone. Logging in over the telephone is as easy as logging in to your Internet provider is with your computer. Using the tone buttons on your telephone you enter your account ID number and then your password. Anyone can access voice mail logging in as public user. Or if you forget your account ID number, you can just type in your surname using the numbers that correspond to the letters on the telephone. Like an answering machine, voice mail takes messages and automatically switches on if you don't answer the phone. But, like e-mail, it can forward those messages anywhere in the world in mere minutes.

Imagine you are a manager with 10 traveling sales people. You could send all of them the details of their next appointment without having to talk to them personally. The salesmen would call into the voice mail system and pick up messages you just sent them wherever they are. All they ever need is a phone.

Welcome to CyberChat

The International Relay Channel, or IRC, is the online place where people from all over the world get together to talk in real time. Think of it as a giant party line where words are typed instead of spoken. You can interview potential employees, conduct meetings, even conference with branches of your company in other parts of the world. These meetings and interviews usually take place in a channel. IRC has over 2,000 channels at any given time. If the one you need or are interested in is not there, all you need to do is create it. If all of this is making you feel disoriented and lost in cyberspace, take heart. It isn't as difficult as it sounds.

Chatting on IRC takes the form of typing on your computer. Imagine you are a manager at IBM for 20 salespersons located in different parts of the country. You want to discuss a new product with them and decide to use IRC as the vehicle for a product information meeting. Connecting to IRC is easy. First you would log in by entering your username and password. Once you are on the Internet, you connect to IRC, usually by clicking on the IRC icon. Once you are on, you simply type the name of the channel you wish to join, for example, /join #IBM. Or, start a new channel by typing, /join #newsales. You can make this channel private by typing the proper command; in this instance, /mode #newsales +p. Or, make it so people can come in by invitation only by typing /mode #newsales +i.

The cost of all this hi-tech virtual business is the price of a computer, a modem and a phone connection which is a lot less than office space rent. Imagine the time and space savings your company would realize by accessing today's most valuable high-tech tool, the Internet. You are a phone call away from equipping your company with the latest, fastest-growing communications tool.

Key Concepts in Chapter 12

- The Internet includes all of cyberspace. It is a network that links computers all over the world.

- E-mail is electronic mail. Correspondence gets from one place to another in a matter of minutes.

- E-mail allows you to read mail, send mail and attach files from anywhere in your word processing program. You can send carbon copies and forward mail to as many persons in as many places all over the world as needed by just typing in their e-mail addresses.

- A fax machine allows you to send facsimiles of anything you have on paper including diagrams and legal documents.

- The major advantage of faxing over e-mail is that you send a fax to a machine, but you have to send e-mail to a computer.

- Voice mail allows you to send a message to anyone anywhere in the world wherever they are that they can pick up when they get to the nearest phone.

- On Internet Relay Chat (IRC) you can interview potential employees and conduct meetings or even conference with branches of your company in other parts of the world in real time.

1. Imagine you were one of the first settlers, a pioneer on the frontier. Consider if you will the new frontier, the Internet. Millions of doors all over the world have opened to you. Get excited, get inspired, but whatever you get, get on the Internet! Be patient with yourself, though. The West wasn't won overnight. Allot a certain amount of time each week for learning the Internet. In three years, it will be as common in every home as the television.

2. The future is now. Imagine earth from outer space, held in a web-like image formed by a vast network of computer cables. We are all connected. Human communication has soared to new heights never before imagined.

   As we connect together all over the globe, there is an air of expectancy, a pause of consideration and wonder. The communication possibilities are limitless.

Reflections

INDEX

Buy any 3, get 1 FREE!

Get a 60-Minute Training Series™ Handbook FREE ($14.95 value) when you buy any three. See back of order form for full selection of titles. These are helpful how-to books for you, your employees and co-workers. Add to your library. Use for new-employee training, brown-bag seminars, promotion gifts and more. Choose from many popular titles on a variety of lifestyle, communication, productivity and leadership topics. Exclusively from National Press Publications.

DESKTOP HANDBOOK ORDER FORM

Ordering is easy:

1. Complete both sides of this order form, detach, and mail, fax or phone your order to:

   Mail: National Press Publications
   6901 W. 63rd St.
   P.O. Box 2949
   Shawnee Mission, KS 66201-1349

   Fax: 1-913-432-0824

   Phone: 1-800-258-7248 (in Canada 1-800-685-4142)

2. Please print:

Name _____ Position/Title _____

Company/Organization _____

Address _____ City_____

State/Province_____ ZIP/Postal Code_____

Telephone(____) _____ Fax (____) _____

3. Easy payment:

❏ Enclosed is my check or money order for $_____ (total from back).
Please make payable to National Press Publications.

Please charge to:
❏ MasterCard   ❏ VISA   ❏ American Express

Credit Card No. _____ Exp. Date _____

Signature _____

• •

MORE WAYS TO SAVE:

SAVE 34%!!! BUY 20-50 COPIES of any title ... pay just $8.97 each ($11.18 Canadian).
SAVE 42%!!! BUY 51 COPIES OR MORE of any title ... pay just $8.69 each ($9.85 Canadian).

Buy 3, get 1 FREE!
60-MINUTE TRAINING SERIES™ HANDBOOKS

TITLE	RETAIL PRICE	QTY.	TOTAL
8 Steps for Highly Effective Negotiations #424	$14.95		
Assertiveness #442	$14.95		
Balancing Career and Family #415	$14.95		
Change: Coping with Tomorrow Today #421	$14.95		
Customer Service: The Key ... Customers #488	$14.95		
Empowering the Self-Directed Team #422	$14.95		
Fear &-Anger: Slay the Dragons ... #4302	$14.95		
Getting Things Done #411	$14.95		
How to Conduct Win-Win Perf. Appraisals #423	$14.95		
How to Find Your Way Around the Internet #4305	$14.95		
How to Manage Conflict #495	$14.95		
How to Manage Your Boss #493	$14.95		
Listen Up: Hear What's Really Being Said #4172	$14.95		
Diversity — Managing Our Differences #412	$14.95		
Master Microsoft Word #406	$14.95		
Motivation and Goal-Setting #4962	$14.95		
A New Attitude #4432	$14.95		
PC Survival Guide #407	$14.95		
Parenting: Ward & June ... #486	$14.95		
Peak Performance #469	$14.95		
Powerful Communication Skills #4132	$14.95		
The Polished Professional #426	$14.95		
The Power of Innovative Thinking #428	$14.95		
Powerful Leadership Skills for Women #463	$14.95		
Powerful Presentation Skills #461	$14.95		
Real Men Don't Vacuum #416	$14.95		
Self-Esteem: The Power to Be Your Best #4642	$14.95		
SELF Profile #403	$14.95		
The Stress Management Handbook #4842	$14.95		
Supreme Teams: How to Make Teams Work #4303	$14.95		
The Supervisor's Handbook #410	$14.95		
Team-Building #494	$14.95		
Techniques to Improve Your Writing Skills #460	$14.95		
The Windows Handbook #4303	$14.95		

Sales Tax
All purchases subject to state and local sales tax.
Questions?
Call
1-800-258-7248

Subtotal	$
Add 7% Sales Tax *(Or add appropriate state and local tax)*	$
Shipping and Handling *($1 one item; 50¢ each additional item)*	$

Buy any 3, get 1 FREE!

BUY 3 GET 1 FREE!
Buy more, save more!

Get a 60-Minute Training Series™ Handbook FREE ($14.95 value)
when you buy any three. See back of order form for full selection of titles.
These are helpful how-to books for you, your employees and co-workers. Add
to your library. Use for new-employee training, brown-bag seminars, promotion gifts
and more. Choose from many popular titles on a variety of lifestyle, communication,
productivity and leadership topics. Exclusively from National Press Publications.

DESKTOP HANDBOOK ORDER FORM

Ordering is easy:

1. Complete both sides of this order form, detach, and mail, fax or phone your order to:

      Mail: National Press Publications
               6901 W. 63rd St.
               P.O. Box 2949
               Shawnee Mission, KS 66201-1349

  Fax: 1-913-432-0824

  Phone: 1-800-258-7248 (in Canada 1-800-685-4142)

2. Please print:

Name _____ Position/Title _____

Company/Organization _____

Address _____ City_____

State/Province_____ ZIP/Postal Code _____

Telephone(____) _____   Fax (____) _____

3. Easy payment:

❑ Enclosed is my check or money order for $_____ (total from back).
Please make payable to National Press Publications.

Please charge to:
❑ MasterCard   ❑ VISA   ❑ American Express

Credit Card No. _____ Exp. Date _____

Signature _____

• •

MORE WAYS TO SAVE:

SAVE 34%!!! BUY 20-50 COPIES of any title ... pay just $8.97 each ($11.18 Canadian).
SAVE 42%!!! BUY 51 COPIES OR MORE of any title ... pay just $8.69 each ($9.85 Canadian).

Buy 3, get 1 FREE!
60-MINUTE TRAINING SERIES™ HANDBOOKS

TITLE	RETAIL PRICE	QTY.	TOTAL
8 Steps for Highly Effective Negotiations #424	$14.95		
Assertiveness #442	$14.95		
Balancing Career and Family #415	$14.95		
Change: Coping with Tomorrow Today #421	$14.95		
Customer Service: The Key ... Customers #488	$14.95		
Empowering the Self-Directed Team #422	$14.95		
Fear &-Anger: Slay the Dragons ... #4302	$14.95		
Getting Things Done #411	$14.95		
How to Conduct Win-Win Perf. Appraisals #423	$14.95		
How to Find Your Way Around the Internet #4305	$14.95		
How to Manage Conflict #495	$14.95		
How to Manage Your Boss #493	$14.95		
Listen Up: Hear What's Really Being Said #4172	$14.95		
Diversity — Managing Our Differences #412	$14.95		
Master Microsoft Word #406	$14.95		
Motivation and Goal-Setting #4962	$14.95		
A New Attitude #4432	$14.95		
PC Survival Guide #407	$14.95		
Parenting: Ward & June ... #486	$14.95		
Peak Performance #469	$14.95		
Powerful Communication Skills #4132	$14.95		
The Polished Professional #426	$14.95		
The Power of Innovative Thinking #428	$14.95		
Powerful Leadership Skills for Women #463	$14.95		
Powerful Presentation Skills #461	$14.95		
Real Men Don't Vacuum #416	$14.95		
Self-Esteem: The Power to Be Your Best #4642	$14.95		
SELF Profile #403	$14.95		
The Stress Management Handbook #4842	$14.95		
Supreme Teams: How to Make Teams Work #4303	$14.95		
The Supervisor's Handbook #410	$14.95		
Team-Building #494	$14.95		
Techniques to Improve Your Writing Skills #460	$14.95		
The Windows Handbook #4303	$14.95		

Sales Tax All purchases subject to state and local sales tax. Questions? Call **1-800-258-7248**	**Subtotal**	$
	Add 7% Sales Tax *(Or add appropriate state and local tax)*	$
	Shipping and Handling *($1 one item; 50¢ each additional item)*	$